BIG PAW

Eugenia Yeuell
Illustrated by Mernie Gallagher-Cole

Rigby

Big Paw lived in a house with a big backyard. She loved to play wildcat.

Big Paw played like she was a lioness.
She hid in the grass.
"I'm hunting for my dinner,"
roared Big Paw.

She jumped to catch the animal.
It was a grasshopper.
It hopped away.

Big Paw went to the birdbath.
An animal was drinking.
"I'm hunting for my dinner,"
roared Big Paw.

She ran to catch the animal.
It was a squirrel.
It ran away.

Big Paw climbed a tree.
She saw two birds.

Big Paw climbed higher to catch them.
They flew away.

"Hunting is hard work," thought Big Paw. "I need a nap."

Big Paw dreamed wildcat dreams.

Then Big Paw heard her name.
"Big Paw, come down for dinner,"
called the children.

Big Paw ran to the children.
She purred and purred.
Then she ate her dinner.

"This is better than hunting," thought Big Paw.